essential careers™

CAREERS IN
JANITORIAL AND CLEANING SERVICES

DON RAUF

ROSEN
PUBLISHING

NEW YORK

Published in 2015 by The Rosen Publishing Group, Inc.
29 East 21st Street, New York, NY 10010

Copyright © 2015 by The Rosen Publishing Group, Inc.

First Edition

Library of Congress Cataloging-in-Publication Data

Rauf, Don.
Careers in janitorial and cleaning services/Don Rauf.—First edition.
     p. cm.—(Essential careers)
Includes bibliographical references and index.
Audience: Grade 7–12.
ISBN 978-1-4777-7880-7 (library bound)
1. Building cleaning industry—Vocational guidance—Juvenile literature.
2. Janitors—Supply and demand—Juvenile literature. I. Title.
HD9999.B882R38 2015
648'.5023—dc23

2014012127

Manufactured in the United States of America

contents

INTRODUCTION   4

CHAPTER 1: CLEANING UP IN THE WORLD OF

      JANITORIAL SERVICES   7

CHAPTER 2: WHAT IS THE JOB REALLY LIKE?   19

CHAPTER 3: GETTING STARTED   32

CHAPTER 4: ADVANCING IN THE JANITORIAL

      UNIVERSE   44

CHAPTER 5: THE LATEST DEVELOPMENTS IN

      JANITORIAL SERVICES   57

GLOSSARY   67

FOR MORE INFORMATION   69

FOR FURTHER READING   72

BIBLIOGRAPHY   74

INDEX   77

INTRO

Janitorial and cleaning services careers are often thought to be "recession-proof." Businesses always need cleaning professionals no matter how well the economy is doing.

DUCTION

Do you like talking dirt? If you literally like thinking about how to get things cleaned up and looking good, a career in janitorial and cleaning services might be for you. It might not be the most glamorous field, but these are essential services that are always needed by businesses and homeowners, and it's work in which professional cleaners can take pride. Some might be put off by the title itself, but janitors also go by the titles custodian, facility technician, and building caretaker. Some janitors have gone on to become wealthy entrepreneurs—they're not only cleaning up buildings, but they're cleaning up financially as well. Even when the economy is in a downturn, businesses need skilled janitors to keep workplaces clean and busy professionals hire cleaners to tend to their homes while they're at work.

The good news today is that janitorial opportunities are on the rise—the Bureau of Labor Statistics predicts steady growth over the next ten years. The job can be a stepping-stone to bigger things—some gain the skills to become building maintenance professionals, electricians, or even superintendents of buildings. The career can be perfect for someone who doesn't want to be stuck behind a desk all day. It requires a number of different tasks during the day, many demanding physical exertion.

The job has become more sophisticated over time as cleaning experts need to operate more complex equipment, mix special cleaning fluids, and address specific needs of the business community. (Many companies want their janitorial staff to be aware of "green" practices, using soaps and detergents that are less harmful to the planet and making sure that workers stick to recycling practices.) While the job in general does not require much training, janitors today might learn to use specialized equipment, like wet-and-dry vacuums and pressure washers. Those who want to make themselves most employable might pursue certification in this field, proving they are capable and well-trained.

For those considering a career path in custodial services, it might be inspiring to learn that several famous people have worked as janitors. The horror writer Stephen King held a job as a school janitor, and his time spent cleaning the girls' locker room reportedly served as inspiration for his hit book *Carrie*. When the comedian Jim Carrey was growing up in Ontario, Canada, his father lost his job and money became so tight that his whole family had to live out of a van. At fifteen, he quit school for a while and worked as a janitor to help keep his family afloat. Keanu Reeves, star of *The Matrix*, also worked as a janitor. Self-help author and motivational speaker Tony Robbins might have found his voice and motivation working as a janitor early in his career. The point is, a career in janitorial services is an honorable way to make a living, and while it can be a long rewarding career in itself, it can also be a jumping-off point to other interesting lines of work.

chapter 1

CLEANING UP IN THE WORLD OF JANITORIAL SERVICES

Janitorial work isn't just about cleaning buildings. For some, providing janitorial services has been a means to get ahead financially as well. It turns out there's some good money to be earned by keeping places spic and span.

When Bryson Raver was a college student at Hillsborough Community College in Tampa, Florida, he cleaned offices to make extra money. At nineteen, he basically had his own one-man cleaning company. When he wasn't in class or doing homework, he was busy networking and looking for new clients who needed their businesses tidied at night. During the evenings, Raver was usually hard at work cleaning offices. For a student like Raver, janitorial services can be the perfect set-up because many companies want cleaning to be done after hours when offices are empty.

Raver was so good at getting new clients, he couldn't handle all the work himself. He gave his operation the name Superior Cleaning Services, and he was soon hiring people to help. Income began to pour in, and in 2007, he made his business official by incorporating it as 360 Facility Services, Inc. As his business grew, he met the owner of a company that provided maintenance for shopping centers, parking garages, and other buildings. The partnership expanded his business even further.

In 2010, Raver's company was big enough to purchase another janitorial services company. As his firm expanded,

Bryson Raver cleaned offices to earn extra money while in college. As he got new clients, he hired others to clean. He eventually became a cleaning services entrepreneur, employing more than 130 people.

Raver moved his operations from his home to a warehouse and office space near Tampa International Airport. The company now has more than 200 clients and employs more than 130 full-time and part-time workers.

His company has been able to attract new customers by advocating "green" cleaning services that involve fewer cleaning agents that cause pollution. In fact, he calls his cleaning process "gleaning"—combining "green" and "clean."

Raver is not the only college student to change buckets of suds into buckets of cash. As a teenager attending college, Mike Moyer also decided to try his hand at the cleaning biz. He had always had an entrepreneurial streak growing up—he had both the classic lemonade stand and a snow-shoveling service.

While in college, he was working a couple of jobs in restaurant service, but he wanted to work for himself. He decided to start a cleaning company because he wanted a business that had very low startup costs as well as minimal monthly expenses.

"Working in my dorm, I filed all the paperwork, set up a corporation, made a website, embroidered some shirts, printed flyers and business cards, and purchased a vacuum and mop bucket," Moyers wrote on his blog. "With less than $400 into the business, I hit the streets looking for customers."

A few offices decided to give Moyers a try. He then landed a big contract with Wal-Mart doing construction cleanup. He teamed up with a friend to expand the business. Through a personal connection, the two were able to get a contract cleaning one of the biggest churches in West Palm Beach, Florida. For a while, the business earned him and his friend a full-time income, although they became interested in other pursuits and moved on.

Both Moyers and Raver found that there's good money to be made in the cleaning industry.

A CAREER THAT IS ALWAYS IN DEMAND

The cleaning business is one that will never go away. People always need their workplaces and homes cleaned—and they don't always want to do it themselves.

The janitorial services field is certainly devoted to doing a lot about cleaning. Janitors mop, scrub, and vacuum floors. They gather and empty trash. They service, clean, and supply restrooms—and let's face it, ridding a toilet of muck or unclogging a sink of debris can be unpleasant, but it is only a portion of the job. These professionals also clean and polish furniture and fixtures. Equipped with soapy water or other cleaners, sponges, and squeegees, they clean windows, glass partitions, and mirrors. They dust furniture, walls, machines, and equipment.

For more intensive cleaning jobs, they might have to steam-clean or shampoo carpets, or strip, seal, finish, and polish floors. When a building is damaged by fire, smoke, or water, a cleaning expert might be called in to restore interiors.

While many cleaning jobs involve simple soap, buckets, sponges, and rags, others require more sophisticated equipment and machinery, such as carpet shampooers, floor strippers, and polishers.

SELF-QUIZ: IS A CAREER AS A JANITOR FOR YOU?

This yes/no quiz can help you decide if a career as a janitor might be for you. If the majority of your answers are yes, this might be a field worth exploring.

1. Do you like to clean?
2. Do you like keeping things in order?
3. Do you think you'd like a non-desk job?
4. Do you like to help others?
5. Do you like physical work?
6. Are you concerned about the safety and health of others?
7. Do you like to work on your own?
8. Do you think you'd like working at nights, alone?
9. Do you like quiet time?
10. Do you think you'd enjoy work that is relatively low-stress?
11. Are you comfortable working with some heavy equipment?
12. Are you comfortable mixing cleaning solutions?
13. Do you get satisfaction from leaving places better than they were?
14. Do you have an interest in the environment and using "green" products?
15. Do you think you'd enjoy a job that helps prevent the spread of illness?
16. Do you like repairing things?
17. Do you like contributing to the greater good of a group of people?
18. Are you interested in a career that does not require a college education?

19. Would you be willing to take specialized training regarding equipment and safety?

20. Are you interested in doing possible outdoor work, such as moving lawns and shoveling walkways?

21. Can you handle doing repetitive tasks?

22. Do you have good communication and interpersonal skills?

23. Can you follow directions?

24. Do have patience?

25. Are you detail-oriented?

Janitorial work, however, often goes well beyond the world of scrubbing. Work can take some technical smarts, making adjustments and minor repairs to heating, cooling, ventilating, plumbing, and electrical systems. The professionals might need to use detailed techniques involving solvents, brushes, rags, and power-cleaning tools to clean laboratory equipment, such as glassware and metal instruments. Also, chimneys, flues, and connecting pipes might require power and hand tools. Specific procedures might have to be followed using chemical cleaners and power equipment to prevent damage to floors and fixtures.

The job can be physically demanding, moving heavy furniture, equipment, and supplies, either manually or by using hand trucks. Janitors get out of their usual work zone when they drive vehicles required to perform or travel to cleaning work, including vans, industrial trucks, or industrial vacuum cleaners. Some must mow and trim lawns and shrubbery, using mowers and hand and power trimmers, and clearing debris from grounds. When rodents and insects become a nuisance, it's often up to the janitor to spray insecticides and fumigants to rid or prevent infestation.

In winter months, many janitors might go on snow patrol. They clear snow from sidewalks, driveways, and parking areas, using snowplows, snow blowers, and snow shovels. They also spread melting salt and chemicals on icy walkways.

JANITORS WEAR MANY HATS

When special occasions come up, janitors plan and set up decorations, tables, chairs, ladders, and scaffolding to prepare facilities for events such as banquets and meetings. Then, when the party's over, they have to spring back into clean-up mode.

Custodians might also wear the hat of security guard—checking on the building's safety—making sure that doors that should be locked are locked, and keeping an eye out for any suspicious behaviors or criminal activity. They keep a close watch on their building and lock all doors after operating hours.

In addition, these professionals have to be ever vigilant, keeping an eye out for things that need repair. If fire alarms are out of charge, they need to replace batteries. If lights in hallways are out, they need to replace bulbs. If wires are frayed, they need to mend or replace exposed wires that could spark a fire. Keeping all parts of the building in proper working order helps assure the safety of all who use the building.

The janitor also wears the hats of bookkeeper and supply manager. He must make sure he has all

Janitorial careers have grown more sophisticated. For example, many must learn computer programs to manage accounting (costs of materials and labor) and track the inventory of cleaning supplies.

he needs to perform his job, and if he doesn't, he must requisition the supplies and equipment needed for cleaning and maintenance duties.

A GROWING OCCUPATIONAL FIELD

The field of janitorial services is steadily adding jobs. The Bureau of Labor Statistics estimates that employment will rise by 12 percent in the coming years. Many opportunities are expected in the health care industry. As the population ages and medicine advances, facilities to care for the elderly are anticipated to multiply. When it comes to health care, cleanliness is extremely important. In effect, janitors are on the front lines when it comes to preventing the spread of illnesses by keeping many environments disinfected and germ-free.

The Bureau of Labor Statistics reports that just over a third of all janitors were employed by the buildings and dwellings industry, and another 14 percent were employed by elementary and secondary schools. The rest worked throughout various industries.

Opportunities for janitors are wide-reaching. Corporate offices, schools, government buildings, retail stores, movie complexes, malls, recording studios, restaurants, and sports facilities all need a clean-up crew.

Most janitors and building cleaners are employed full-time, but a large number also work part-time, and that can be a major plus for those who also are attending school or raising a family. Because office buildings are often cleaned while empty, many cleaners work evening hours. For some, it can be a solitary job, working the night shift after the day workers have gone home. But that can suit many just fine who might like to have time to themselves, mopping the hallways while listening to music on an iPod, for example.

Cleaning services often suit those who enjoy working alone. Many duties are performed at night when workers are away from the office. Cleaners may listen to music and complete tasks without interacting with other people.

Still, many janitorial positions require day work—schools, for example, might expect custodians to be on hand to take care of cleaning and maintenance tasks that come up during the course of the day. Hospital and hotels might require twenty-four-hour maintenance staff, and janitors are typically assigned shifts to make sure around-the-clock service is provided.

You might not think of the job as one for risk-takers, but building cleaners have one of the highest rates of injuries and illnesses of all occupations, according to the Bureau of Labor Statistics. Machines, tools, and chemicals can cause minor cuts, bruises, and burns. Workers have to take care not to overexert themselves or they might suffer an injury, such as a strained back. More and more, janitors receive training ergonomics, which is a science that deals with designing and arranging things so that people can use their work tools easily and safely and approach tasks in such a way that will be least stressful or potentially harmful to their bodies. Repetitive tasks, such as mopping and wringing, can lead to aches, pain, and numbness in the neck, arms, and hands. Lifting heavy items might strain the back.

Many of these professionals take safety-training instruction as well. Janitors need to know how to recognize and deal with chemical hazards, electrical hazards, slips and falls, emergencies like fires and floods, and robberies and assaults. Janitors working alone at night might face risks regarding crime. Electrical equipment has the potential to cause harmful shocks if not handled appropriately. Toxins found in cleaning supplies can cause eye irritation, skin rashes, coughing and respiratory problems, dizziness, and more serious health issues.

chapter 2

WHAT IS THE JOB
REALLY LIKE?

The janitor's role is more than just mopping and sweeping. Janitors really are responsible for keeping a building in top condition. Because they take a building under their care, they're often called custodians or maintenance workers. Their job is more than just cleaning and removing trash. In fact, some custodians are responsible for so many different things that no day on the job is the same.

A VARIETY OF TASKS

Janitors often operate large vacuum cleaners and floor polishers. More intensive work might involve cleaning heavy machinery; tending furnaces, air conditioners, and boilers; and operating heavy machinery, such as paper balers.

They might be responsible for simple electrical and plumbing repairs. They also replace light bulbs or fix and replace door locks. If they advance, they could service a building's heating and air-conditioning system. A custodian might direct how furniture is set up in an office and supervise disposal of old furniture and other large-scale items.

On a typical day, janitors might clean office floors, walls, and windows. Glass partitions and mirrors are also on the list. Some items, like door handles and knobs, are easily overlooked, but a custodian has to remember to scrub these as well, since

Janitorial work can go beyond cleaning. Many professionals are responsible for simple plumbing and electronic repairs, such as repairing a light fixture. These duties can require the use of simple hand tools.

these can be surfaces that spread germs. Some days, cleaning might be lighter. Furniture, machines, and equipment often need dusting. Janitors might spend time mopping the hallways and inside restrooms.

Janitors make sure they come to each cleaning site fully equipped with the necessary supplies and tools. They often bring soapy water, cleaning fluids, sponges, and squeegees. Since a top-notch cleanup person has the right tools and supplies at the ready, those in custodial work perform regular checks on their supplies, noting when cleaning solutions and other solutions are running low so that they can be sure to reorder before they are fresh out.

Keeping track of inventory most likely requires some computer savvy, often working with spreadsheets and Excel files to track quantities, prices, and ordering status. Janitors might be given a budget as well, so they might have to shop around with various suppliers to pinpoint the most cost-effective materials.

WORKING WITH OTHERS

Attitude can make all the difference on the job. One school janitor interviewed online said he treated his janitorial work as an art. He worked a broom with the grace of Fred Astaire. He prided himself that when you entered a room after he cleaned it, you would not smell a thing.

As the gatekeeper for the building or facility where they work, janitors have a sense of who is coming and going. Often when packages or furniture are delivered, the janitor directs items to their proper location, particularly in smaller businesses.

While the work can often be completed alone, janitors might have to interact with many people in a building, from visitors asking directions to managers who need to review what cleanup and maintenance needs to be taken care of in the days

TOOLS OF THE TRADE

If you're stepping into the arena of janitorial work, you'll need to familiarize yourself with some of the basic tools of the trade to do successful battle with dirt, dust, grease, and grime.

- •Upright vacuum. An essential device for keeping floors free of dust and dirt.

- •Broom and dustpan. The dropped and smashed bottle, food spilled in the common eating area, coffee grounds dumped on the floor—for the little accidents, the age-old combination of broom and dustpan is key.

- •Bucket. Soap and water and other cleaning solutions are typically mixed in a standard bucket.

- •Terry cloth rags. For the fast wipe-up, a terry cloth rag can be just the thing. Terry cloth is extra absorbent.

- •Cotton, smooth, white rags (non-terry) for dusting. When the dust settles, the cotton rags need to come out.

- •Personal protection items, such as rubber gloves, aprons, coveralls, and dust masks. Fumes from cleaning solutions, matter in the air from cleaning, and other harsh ingredients that come in contact with the skin can all affect a person's health. To avoid bodily trouble during cleaning duties, janitors put on protective gear.

- •Furniture polish without wax in it (to avoid buildup). A shiny office is an impressive office, and employers appreciate the custodian who keeps woodwork buffed.

- •Glass cleaner. Cooped up in an office all day, workers look out their windows for a break. Keeping the glass clean can be a morale booster.

TOOLS OF THE TRADE

- Paper towels. Don't take paper towels for granted. They're often the right supply for the job.

- Bathtub and basin cleaner. Sinks and tubs often require the extra scrubbing agent to get rid of soap buildup and grime.

- Hard-water stain remover. This is a very specific agent used for one targeted task.

- Bags in which to keep clean rags and dirty rags. Sometimes organization is the key, and a cleaning crewmember needs to have rags at the ready.

- Floor cleaner. Floors can get especially filthy from the feet of the masses tracking in mud and muck, scuffs from shoes, or marks from equipment that must be wheeled through hallways. Cleaning agents powerful enough to scrub floors are a must.

- Phone to make and receive calls. Quick: Cleanup on the fifth floor! Sometimes a janitor's services are required right away, and he or she needs to be reached quickly. Most carry a cell phone so that they can respond in a flash to emergency spills.

ahead. In some cases, janitors might report directly to an office manager or school principal.

Therefore, janitors should look clean and presentable and be able to communicate with others. They should be friendly and courteous to the people who work in the building or students attending the school, as well as any visitors to the site.

They also must be able to get along with other janitors. Although custodians are often told what to do, they might have

To perform dirty work, professionals may wear clothes that are made to get dirty, such as special smocks, jumpsuits, and overalls. Many are designed with pockets big enough to carry cleaning supplies.

to supervise a staff and instruct coworkers on proper techniques. It is important that they are able to receive and carry out instructions, and that they communicate tasks to others in a way that will motivate them.

LOCATION IS EVERYTHING

Cleaning duties often depend on the type of workplace. Janitors work in airports, auto showrooms, convention centers, retail stores, hotels, universities, hospitals, manufacturing plants, and many other distinct types of business.

Janitors at a pastry factory might face a quarter-inch layer of flour on the floor at the end of each workday that needs to be swept up. Janitors at athletic clubs have to be concerned with cleaning equipment, as well as locker rooms and showers. The opportunities for germs to spread at a gym are many. Sports club janitors often take care of cleaning towels, too, and they might be in charge of maintaining the pool, assuring proper chlorine balance.

Janitors might have to follow very detailed cleaning instructions. For example, they might be put in charge of cleaning recording equipment at a recording studio, which can be crucial for capturing sounds in the best possible way. Besides, you never know where such as job might lead. Trent Reznor of Nine Inch Nails got time to record and became an assistant engineer at Cleveland's Right Track Studio because of connections he made there while working as a janitor. Studio owner Bart Koster reportedly said, "He was so focused in everything he did. When that guy waxed the floor, it looked great." Eventually, Reznor convinced Koster to give him unused studio time to record his original music.

In an industrial setting, the work can be heavy duty to eliminate lint, dust, oil, and grease from machines and conveyers.

JANITOR RÉSUMÉ TIPS

Once a janitor gets some work under his or her belt, these tips might help in shaping a résumé:

1. Highlight the numbers. Janitors can give an employer an idea of their capabilities by detailing how many offices they were in charge of cleaning or the size of spaces that he or she cleaned. For example, a hotel janitor might say that he or she cleaned more than 300 hotel rooms, representing about 140 customers per day.

2. Show leadership. Janitors might underscore any role they had in leadership. For example, if a janitor was in charge of two other people cleaning, that's an impressive detail.

3. Detail accomplishments. If construction, electrical work, or plumbing were part of the job, make sure to explain what those jobs were and that they were completed.

4. Present special talents. Janitors who have experience with specific equipment and power tools need to mention these unique skills on their résumé. A unique talent might also be the ability to speak Spanish and English. These qualities that set a candidate apart can help land him or her a job.

5. List training. In addition to listing the standard high school and college education information, janitors need to present any training that pertains to maintenance and cleaning services. For example, if a janitor holds a certificate in heating, venting, air-conditioning, and refrigeration (HVAC/R), that credential has to be on the résumé.

These specialists wash floors, often using high-powered hoses to clean processing tanks, containers, or barrels.

In a scientific laboratory, cleaning crews might be specially trained in the proper soaps, solvents, and brushes to wash glassware, metal instruments, sinks, tables, and test panels. Careful mixing of water, detergents, and even acids might be required to sanitize test tubes and equipment.

Love sports? You might look into a custodial position with a sports stadium or arena. You might be sweeping up popcorn, picking up trash, and mopping up soda spills, but you might also have the fringe benefit of being able to see a game for free.

Maybe you're a movie and television fan. All the studios need janitors, and these positions put cleaning staff on the front lines to see celebrities up close and in person as they film their scenes.

Love pets? Try the local veterinarian's office. Maybe fashion is your thing. Studios that design clothes certainly need cleanup crews, as do art studios. For many janitors, working in an environment that holds special interest for them can give a job that extra appeal.

Some might enjoy the peace, quiet, and reflection of working as a caretaker at a church, synagogue, or temple. Hospitals can be very particular about how their facilities are cleaned and disinfected. An article in *Scientific American* highlights how some hospitals are investing more money in janitorial staffs because a growing number of patients were becoming difficult to treat and falling victim to infections. Microorganisms that spread infection and disease can live on different types of surfaces unless they are properly cleaned. Bacteria can be hardy, surviving on bed rails, shower curtains, and keyboards. Some medical facilities have struggled with the spread of MRSA, or methicillin-resistant *Staphylococcus aureus*, which causes a drug-resistant staph infection.

Those in the cleaning biz may find an employer that matches their interests. Janitors find work in sports arenas, veterinarian offices, hospitals, recording studios, clothing design firms, and more.

Many illnesses are spread by hand-to-hand contact, and custodians play a role here as well, making sure that soap and towel dispensers are fully stocked. Hospitals depend on their building service crews to help eliminate bacteria and reduce the chances of infections. In many institutions, cleaning staff might not have been treated as serious members of the operations teams. They were seen as easily replaceable, and that type of attitude can cause cleanliness to suffer.

At New York University's Langone Medical Center, a program was launched that teamed a cleaning crew with infection-control specialists and nurses so that they could develop the most effective approaches for sanitizing. The hospital reported that within the first six months of starting the "clean team" program, the occurrence of infections dropped dramatically. Now these clean teams are regularly assigned to clean acute-care beds throughout the hospital.

Certain cleaning careers can be very specialized. Eileen de Jager and Roelien Schutte (pictured here) *make a living cleaning up crime scenes. Because all bodily fluids are considered biohazards, they must dispose of them with great care.*

There are obviously specialties when it comes to the cleaning industry. One niche worth mentioning is crime-scene cleanup. We all see TV shows where there are bloody crime scenes, but the shows rarely depict those who have specialized skills in cleaning up that type of mess. Deborah and Charles Moore are a married couple and a crime-cleaning duo. They run their own business called Crime Clean of Texas, scrubbing up locations after suicides and violent murders.

chapter 3

GETTING STARTED

Janitorial services is a field that a young person can start to explore now. A smart first step is to get some practice cleaning your own home. Your parents certainly will not mind if you volunteer to vacuum, dust, and clean the bathrooms. A young person might even be able to negotiate getting some extra money from the folks in return for making things fresh and clean around the house. Also, the experience allows a novice janitor the chance to find out what products work best and how to most efficiently clean different rooms.

With some cleaning experience under their belt, teenagers can branch out and explore more opportunities. One approach is to print flyers and offer cleaning services to neighbors and neighborhood businesses. The heads of households often can be too busy taking care of their own work matters to find time to clean, so they might be very willing to employ a young person to vacuum, scrub toilets, and wash the dishes.

Managers of local businesses and institutions might also be willing to employ a young person to clean their offices. Dawn Loggins found a job with her high school in Lawndale, North Carolina, through the school workforce assistance program. Dawn has had an especially difficult time in school because, at age seventeen, her drug-abusing parents abandoned her and left her homeless. She grew up in a home that often didn't have electricity or running water. She and her brother often brought water home in jugs from the public park. To make money, she

You can often start doing janitorial work at a young age. High school student Dawn Loggins found employment as a custodian at her school in Lawndale, North Carolina, getting there before sunrise to sweep classrooms.

HOW TO SUCCEED IN BUSINESS

If you want to do well in custodial services, remember the following:

- **Clean like you're on a hidden camera.** One janitor at a museum lost his job after knocking over a valuable sculpture with his mop. He didn't realize that a security camera caught him in the act. Janitors should clean as if they are being watched because often they are.

- **Take care with expensive items.** In the movie *Mr. Bean*, Rowan Atkinson sneezes on the *Mona Lisa*. He tries to clean it and winds up smudging the paint. Janitors need to keep in mind the material of the objects they are cleaning and the solutions they use on them. In real life, at Dortmund, Germany's Museum Ostwall, a member of the cleaning crew scrubbed away a patina intended to look like a dried rain puddle at the base of artist Martin Kippenberger's *When It Starts Dripping from the Ceiling*. What she thought was a stain was actually an integral part of the million-dollar artwork. The lesson: A work of art needs to be cleaned in a very specific manner by specialists. Follow the rules spelled out by your employer.

- **Offer services that are above and beyond.** The janitors that get recognized and rewarded do more than the expected. They might offer to wash windows, clean up after pets, or run errands. When janitors offer more, they become more valued.

- **Be prompt.** Show up on time every day to work or even a little early. Don't leave just as the clock hits quitting time.

- **Use downtime productively.** When there are not immediate tasks to be taken care of, think of things that should be done to improve the work environment or tasks that haven't been assigned but will help coworkers. Take initiative and do those

How to Succeed in Business

tasks no one else wants to do. For example, take time to clean and organize the supply closet. Ask your boss if there are other tasks beyond the usual that need to be done.

- **Be flexible.** If something comes up that isn't on the list of expected chores, take it on. Try to be flexible and don't say, "Sorry, that's not my job."

- **Mind your manners.** Good manners make good impressions. Always say "please" and "thank you," just as you were taught growing up.

- **Dress neatly.** Janitors don't need to be snappy dressers, but keeping a neat appearance makes a good impression with all in the workplace.

- **Be respectful.** Coworkers are willing to help the person more who shows them respect.

- **Ask for help.** When you don't understand something, don't be afraid to ask. Or if a job is too big or complicated for one person, ask for backup. Some feel reluctant or embarrassed to ask for help, but they shouldn't.

- **Take breaks.** While you want to work as hard as possible and do a great job, everyone needs some downtime. Too much work can overtire and overstress a person and prevent one from working up to his or her best potential.

- **Keep things neat.** Keeping a workplace and supplies neat and organized makes work easier. Following systems can also make a task easier to complete.

- **Take credit.** Be sure all your good work gets noticed. Make sure those in charge are aware of your accomplishments and the extra projects you've taken on.

took a job as a custodian at her school. Before the sun even rose, she would clean and sweep all the classrooms, picking gum and litter off the floors. She would complete many of her duties before the first bell rang. Dawn went on to attend Harvard, where she no doubt made use of the responsibility and discipline she developed while working as a janitor.

HUNTING FOR A JOB

While teens can go door-to-door and advertise their services and willingness to work, they can also take advantage of employment services. Many online employment operations will show if there are opportunities locally. SnagaJob (www.snagajob.com), for example, lists teen maintenance janitorial jobs. Websites for Indeed and Manpower also list job openings. Young people might get experience by getting a job with an established cleaning service, like Maid Brigade. ABM Janitorial Services, for example, offers a summer internship program.

Some employers, unions, and government agencies offer training courses for new janitors to hone their skills. Typically, novices will learn at the elbow of a seasoned professional. They start with simple tasks and move on to more complex work.

Those who want to excel in the field will dedicate time to learning about cleaning supplies and what cleaning agents are

There are many ways for teens to find opportunities in the cleaning industry. They may advertise themselves as cleaners, check employment services, or even get an internship with an established business.

JANITOR INTERVIEW QUESTIONS

If you go on an interview to become a janitor, you might hear these questions:

1. Tell me about your work background.

2. Why do you want to work here? What interested you about our company?

3. Why do you want to work as a janitor?

4. What are your biggest strengths?

5. What are your biggest weaknesses?

6. Why did you leave your last job?

7. What are your career goals?

8. How would you describe yourself?

9. How would your coworkers describe you?

10. Why should we hire you?

INTERVIEW MISTAKES

Here are some common mistakes people make when applying for a job:

1. Not dressing appropriately.

2. Not being prepared to answer questions.

3. Not knowing enough about the company to which they are applying.

4. Not turning off cell phones.

JANITOR INTERVIEW MISTAKES

5. Not knowing the interviewer's name.

6. Bringing a coffee or drink to the interview.

7. Not introducing themselves.

8. Showing up late.

9. Not bringing extra copies of their résumé.

10. Not bringing a list of references.

11. Not having questions for the interviewer.

12. Not knowing when to stop talking.

13. Being too negative about their old job.

14. Trying too hard or failing to curb enthusiasm.

used on what materials. For example, certain bathroom cleaners will damage wood. Experience with diluting chemicals and cleaning agents can help.

Age can be a factor when it comes to landing a job. If you are under the age of fourteen, jobs can be scarce. At that age, a young person can babysit, deliver newspapers, do some agricultural work, and houseclean. Check with a school counselor and with child labor laws online to see what type of work is allowed at different ages. The U.S. Department of Labor provides of list of those work tasks that are prohibited for young adults. A janitorial job might require some of these tasks—it just depends on the job. For example, a fourteen- or fifteen-year-old may not work in repair or construction; may not operate or assist in operating power-driven machinery or hoisting apparatus other than typical office machines; may not drive motor vehicles or help a driver; may not load or unload goods on or off trucks, railcars or conveyors, except in very limited circumstances; or may not do any work involving the use of ladders, scaffolds, or similar equipment.

LEARNING THE ROPES

Officially, there is no set educational path to becoming a janitor. A high school diploma or GED is considered the minimal amount of education necessary. A person interested in the field might set up an informal internship or apprenticeship, or just to get a sense of the job, one could "shadow" a janitor throughout his or her workday, taking note of the various tasks performed.

The U.S. Department of Labor states that most employees do not need specialized education for this field, but certain courses and training can help them perform the job better. College and high school courses that improve communication can be of use to a janitor who needs to be able to communicate clearly, both verbally and in writing. Mathematics can help with calculations that might be needed in ordering supplies, handling simple accounting, and mixing cleaning fluids. Technology is part of almost every career nowadays, and janitorial work is no different. Computer competence can help land a job, and a basic course that helps use some fundamental tools, such as Word and Excel, might be of value.

While there is no bachelor's degree in janitorial work, some estimate that more than one hundred thousand janitors hold college degrees of some sort. For specific advanced training, there are certification programs that give workers validation that they have proper skills to provide the highest quality in janitorial services. Investigate certification options such as the Cleaning Industry Management Standard (CIMS) certification from the Worldwide Cleaning Industry Association,

Environmental Services/ Janitorial Training Program

with Learning Supports

CCAC–North Campus

Because janitorial techniques and services have grown increasingly sophisticated, some colleges now offer training programs. Many offer certification, which can be valuable for landing a job.

The first choice for faster results.

www.ccac.edu

formerly known as the International Sanitary Supply Association (ISSA). Look into certifications from the International Janitorial Cleaning Services Association (IJCSA) or several certification choices available from the National Association of Certified Building Contractors (NACBC).

Certifications often help when a professional wants to climb up the career ladder. For example, the International Executive Housekeepers Association has a program to become a certified executive housekeeper (CEH) or registered executive housekeeper (REH), which are highly regarded credentials.

To pass certification exams, students might have to complete online courses or buy course materials and study on their own. If one does not earn a passing grade, the exams usually can be retaken.

Some schools offer specific training in maintenance. For example, the Community College of Allegheny County in Monroeville, Pensylvania, has an Environmental Services/ Janitorial Training Program. There are also professional resources that offer continuing education. American School and University in Overland Park, Kansas, provides webinars on school floor maintenance and lessons on cost, function, comfort, and environmental concerns.

To become a janitorial manager, it's helpful to get business skills that can be learned in a management associate's degree program or a bachelor's degree program in business administration. Some technical and career schools offer janitorial management degree and diploma programs. A two-year management program might teach a range of skills that are useful in business leadership roles. These include problem solving, organizational planning, and customer service. General academic coursework in mathematics and writing will help as well.

Graduates of these two-year programs leave with an understanding of basic management principles, business ethics, human resources, marketing, and computers. With more advanced courses, janitors can learn leadership skills, financial management, and operational strategy. College-level courses in management might include microeconomics, macroeconomics, strategic decision-making, and operations management.

Not surprisingly, the annual average salary for house-keeping and janitorial managers and supervisors was higher than annual earnings for janitors and cleaners. Some opportunities require that janitors be union members, and union memberships can mean higher wages. Consult the Bureau of Labor Statistics (http://www.bls.gov) to find out current averages for these professions.

chapter 4

ADVANCING IN THE JANITORIAL UNIVERSE

The title of "janitor" sometimes has a negative connotation, but it actually comes from the Latin word *Janus*, which means "gatekeeper." It's an important position to be the one who "keeps the gate" and presents the building to all who enter. While the position of janitor is valued and essential in its own right, a janitorial job can also be a stepping-stone to more advanced careers in building maintenance and repair. Many janitors go on to become electricians, plumbers, HVAC (heating, ventilation, and air-conditioning) experts, or furnace repairmen.

A CHANCE TO LEARN ELECTRICAL WORK AND PLUMBING

Janitors have opportunities to learn so much more than how to push a broom down a hallway. Appliances break down and electrical problems might arise in any building with regards to outlets, lighting, computers, and more.

To get basic skills in electrical maintenance, one might want to investigate courses in basic electrical engineering at technical schools or community colleges. Many institutions offer training in electricity fundamentals that can be applied in a janitor's work environment. A solid program will start with an introduction to basic electricity fundamentals, how circuits work, and electromagnetism. Look for programs that give hands-on skills in basic wiring and repair. In the world of building maintenance, there are plenty of overloads, fuses, circuit breakers, switches, and other control circuit components that might cause problems.

Consider exploring books on home improvement as well. There are often volumes dedicated to simple home electricity repairs. This can be a good starting point, and many lessons will apply in the workplace, too.

With the right training, a janitor could repair a fluorescent light or change bearings on an electrical motor. He or she could possibly troubleshoot and repair complex motor control circuits and computer systems.

Janitors often have the opportunity to handle minor plumbing repairs. Some of simplest fixes can be a clogged toilet or slow-draining sink. A simple handyman skill is to learn how to handle a snake, which is spiraled through a clogged pipe to restore water flow. A plunger (made of heavy rubber with good suction power) and a snake are certainly two tools that every janitor should have on hand for emergencies. A janitor also needs to know how to shut off water feeding into sinks, showers, and toilets. Other tools for the plumbing kit are assorted pipe wrenches, an adjustable wrench, and offset screwdrivers, ideal for reaching low-access screws and hard-to-reach places.

Leaky faucets are another common plumbing problem that janitors can fix or learn to fix. Worn-out washers are often the culprit, and with some guidance from a self-help plumbing book or online direction, a janitor can repair a leaky faucet.

If janitors want to learn more about plumbing, they should observe and assist professional plumbers when they are called in to fix the bigger problems. Ultimately, if a janitor is serious about becoming a real electrician or plumber, he or she should contact local unions to get involved in an apprenticeship program.

Janitors have opportunities to develop skills that may even lead to other careers. For example, many handle minor plumbing jobs, learning how to snake clogged pipes and repair leaky faucets.

Classroom study is combined with on-the-job training in apprenticeship programs. Apprentices can be employed and earn a salary while they are apprenticing. An apprenticeship is a time commitment. Typically, one can take five years and eight thousand hours to complete, and then the apprentice must pass a state licensing exam to become a plumber or electrician. Classroom instruction might include drafting, blueprint reading, mathematics, applied physics and chemistry, state code, and other regulations that apply to the industry, and safety training according to Occupational Safety and Health Administration guidelines.

SPECIALTIES IN HVAC AND CARPENTRY

Heating, ventilation, and air-conditioning (HVAC) is a specialty area in which janitors might get some training. If something goes wrong with the HVAC in a building, janitors are often called first to evaluate the problem, and they might make minor repairs and adjustments to the HVAC system.

There are certificate, associate's degree, and bachelor's degree programs in HVAC technology. These programs also teach about refrigeration. HVAC instruction typically covers fundamentals on electricity, heating as fueled by gas and electricity, central forced air systems, furnaces, air-conditioning systems, refrigeration, ventilation, and hot water and steam-heating systems.

Another type of specialty work that janitors might do is small carpentry jobs. Shelves might need to be built. Desks might need to be assembled. A janitor with the right skills might build or knock down a wall or partition. Those with carpentry skills might install doors, hardwood flooring, molding, paneling, skylights, and windows. Roof repair could be on the list as well. To complete such jobs, janitors need to assemble a collection of hand and power tools, including hammers, ladders, levels,

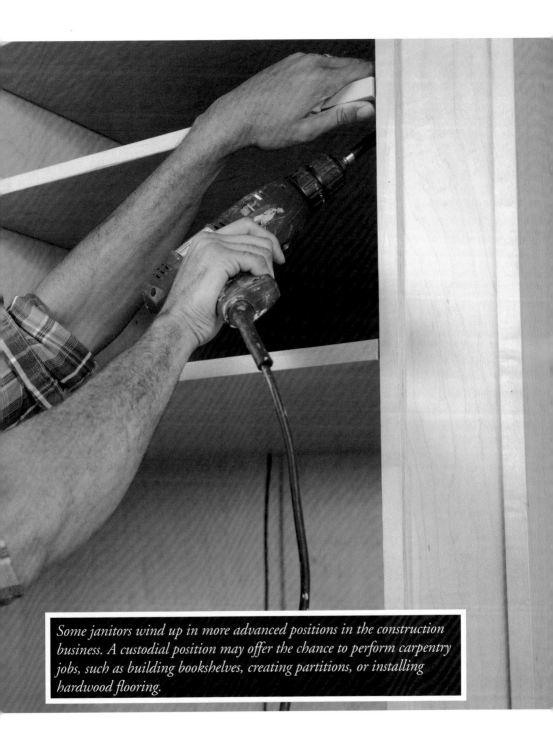

Some janitors wind up in more advanced positions in the construction business. A custodial position may offer the chance to perform carpentry jobs, such as building bookshelves, creating partitions, or installing hardwood flooring.

STARTING YOUR OWN EMPIRE

As you read earlier, some people take their interest in janitorial services and follow an entrepreneurial path. They set up their own janitorial services company. Lawrence Carpenter made a few mistakes early in his life and went to prison. Upon his release, the *Christian Science Monitor* reports that the Durham, North Carolina, native set about the task of starting Super Clean Professional Janitorial Services, a commercial cleaning service. "I wanted something that would get me as far away from the streets as possible, but where there wouldn't be a limit or a cap on how much money I could make." Now the sky seems to be the limit for Carpenter, as Super Clean is generating more than $2.5 million in sales per year and employs more than seventy full-time and part-time employees.

If you want to start your own business, invest in some cleaning supplies and start looking for customers. As you try to get business, it pays to have business cards. Make sure your card features your name, makes it clear that your company is a cleaning service, and provides your phone number and a website address, if you have one.

Before you sell your services, you will need to determine prices. Check out the prices that competitors charge. That will help determine your price and might lead you to set prices lower to be competitive. Think of specials that might win business. For example, consider charging $20 per hour but $15 per hour for six or more hours. Discounts for booking more hours can gain business. You might also try to advertise on websites such as Groupon or Angie's List.

Create a professional-looking flyer to post around town and hand out to businesses. Again, make sure it advertises all the services offered, rates, and contact information. Follow up by making phone calls to all the businesses that received the flyer.

STARTING YOUR OWN EMPIRE

Before getting on the phone, prepare a short pitch. Make sure to have all the information you need to convey by the phone, ready for you to reference while you're talking. And practice before making that first call.

Set goals of how many businesses to call a day. Maintain patience and be ready for rejection. It might take many, many calls before landing a client or two. A real estate office might be a good target because it might need to hire a cleaning service for its properties or clients.

power saws, screwdrivers, and tape measures. Air-quality testing devices are also needed for building maintenance to make sure there are no harmful gases or pollutants in the building. A janitor-carpenter needs to be able to read and understand blueprints, sketches, and building plans.

FOLLOW YOUR INTERESTS

Those who enjoy working outdoors might find they can shift into a career as a groundskeeper, gardener, or landscaper. They might mow lawns, control and install the watering system, trim and fertilize plants, and design how the plant life surrounding a structure should be arranged.

The path of a janitor can develop according to an individual's abilities and interests. Seventeen years ago, Larry Haines began working as the janitor at the Cadillac Wexford Public Library in Michigan. He enjoyed the job, but he also took on additional responsibilities of fixing the computers and showed a real knack for it. Haines is now the technology director, maintaining seventy computers and three servers for the main library and four branch libraries.

For those who want to take on more of a leadership role, a janitor can advance to become a building operations and facilities manager or superintendent. A big office or residential building can receive many requests a day for maintenance and repair. The manager or superintendent has to field all the requests and organize with staff how these matters will

Those with leadership ability may work their way up the career ladder and get managerial positions as building superintendents or building operations and facilities managers.

be handled. Planning and budgeting is key to the job, and typically managers and superintendents might be involved with hiring as well. Facilities managers should have an interest in architecture, interior design, and eco-friendly building practices. A business communication background and organizational skills are essential, as managers and superintendents must often balance different projects while interacting with a number of teams.

RISING TO THE TOP

It doesn't happen often, but janitors might be surprised to learn that they can even rise to the level of corporate executive. Working day-in and day-out in an organization, janitors can learn a lot about a business operation and the people who work there. Richard Montañez is a great example.

In 1976, he was working as a janitor at a Frito-Lay plant in Rancho Cucamonga, California. He did not have a college degree or even a high school diploma. He liked the Cheetos snack food that Frito-Lay manufactured, but he thought Cheetos could use a little kick. In his spare time, he concocted a spicy hot recipe featuring chili powder. He made a few homemade batches of his new spicy Cheetos and tried them out on friends and family. With their approval, Montañez decided to call the chief executive officer of the company. The CEO was intrigued by the idea and invited him to give a presentation.

Richard Montañez is now a top vice president at PepsiCo, but he started at the company as a janitor. He took initiative and presented ideas for new products, which propelled him into an executive position.

With little time to prepare, Montañez checked out a few books on marketing from the public library. He neatly put his chips in sample bags, and he bought his first tie—a $3 special. His presentation was a hit. The CEO and others in management loved his idea, and Flamin' Hot Cheetos were born. This flavor has become one of the company's top sellers. Montañez has risen in the ranks and is today the executive vice president of multicultural sales and community activation for Pepsico, Frito-Lay's parent company. Montañez has said that he rose to the top because he had a Ph.D.—he was "poor, hungry and determined." He also looks back as his career as a janitor as a gateway to great things. "There's no such thing as 'just a janitor,' if you act like an owner," Montañez told the MailOnline.

chapter 5

THE LATEST DEVELOPMENTS IN JANITORIAL SERVICES

One might think that janitorial and cleaning services is a field that never changes. While the mop and bucket never go out of style, certain elements of the cleaning industry have entered the twenty-first century, from environmentally correct approaches to sophisticated cleaning equipment.

GREEN CLEANING

Many professionals and business owners in the janitorial field use "green" products and are helping save the environment. Janitors must know the latest green cleaning approaches and how to maximize recycling efforts. Many companies want to do their share to help the environment, and they have their janitors buy toilet paper and paper towels made from recycled paper.

Professionals in this field have to know which cleaning fluids are plant-based, rather than chemical-based. Many cleaning products contain phosphates, chlorine, ammonia, and petroleum distillates. Some contain elements that are suspected to cause cancer, aggravate allergies, or lead to asthma. These toxins can get into the water supply and lead to a host of ecological

As businesses have become more environmentally conscious, cleaning industry professionals have had to learn about "green" cleaning methods, which require products that are less likely to harm the environment.

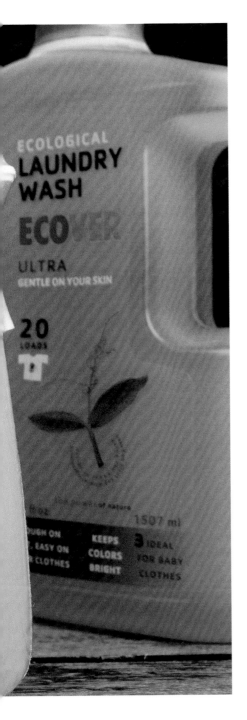

and human health problems. Phosphates, for example, can cause "dead zones" in lakes and streams. Triclosan, a chemical used in antibacterial cleaners, has been shown to interfere with thyroid function in animals.

"Green" brands have proven to do an excellent job at cleaning, and more cleaning products are being developed to meet environmental standards. Some green cleaning products use sustainable coconut palm oil. Some janitors are going back to old-fashioned sustainable cleaning products like distilled white vinegar and baking soda. Cleaning experts might also look for packaging that is easily recyclable, such as cardboard or certain types of plastic.

Professional organizations for janitors often follow the latest developments in cleaning products, and those who want to stay on the cutting edge have to keep up with these items. For example, for years many have thought that antibacterial soaps were necessary to help kill off germs that cause colds and other illnesses. More recent studies have shown that plain old soap and water might do just as good of a job and that the stronger antibacterial soaps might actually be helping to breed a strain of super germ that is resistant to these soaps.

Janitors that do have to use toxic supplies might try to dispose of the wastewater at community facilities that are dedicated to getting rid of harmful waste. When it comes to disposing cleaning products, the best advice is use up as much as possible—don't get rid of it; use it.

The ISSA Worldwide Cleaning Association has a guide to green cleaning products on its website (http://www.issa.com). The organization recommends looking for cleaners that are certified by Green Seal or the Environmental Choice EcoLogo Program.

The use of electrolyzed water is an emerging green cleaning trend. When salt water is subject to electric current, it can produce two solutions—one is a noncorrosive dirt and grease-cutting cleaner (sodium hydroxide) and the other is a highly dissolved oxygen, chlorine-containing sanitizer and disinfectant (hypochlorous acid).

ADVANCED TOOLS OF THE TRADE

Powered cleaning equipment, such as vacuum cleaners, carpet extraction equipment, powered floor maintenance equipment, and scrubbing equipment, can be green as well. Some are more energy-efficient, less noisy, and capture more particulates than others.

As cleaning equipment has grown more sophisticated over the decades, janitors have had to keep up. Today's janitors have to know enhanced vacuum filtration systems; light weight, maneuverable equipment; and specialty equipment.

The International Janitorial Cleaning Services Association published an article on a self-charging robotic vacuum that

The cleaning industry is transforming as new technologies are introduced. A new type of robotic vacuum, for example, is designed to scan the room and then clean it in the most efficient manner.

uses a built-in laser scanner to map the room and plan the most efficient way for cleaning it. Called the BotVac, the device can be turned off in the middle of a job to recharge, and when it returns to the cleaning site, it remembers exactly where it left off.

Hand-dryer technology has come a long way over the years. Old hand blowers in restrooms seemed to give off a faint, distant breeze. People would waste precious time

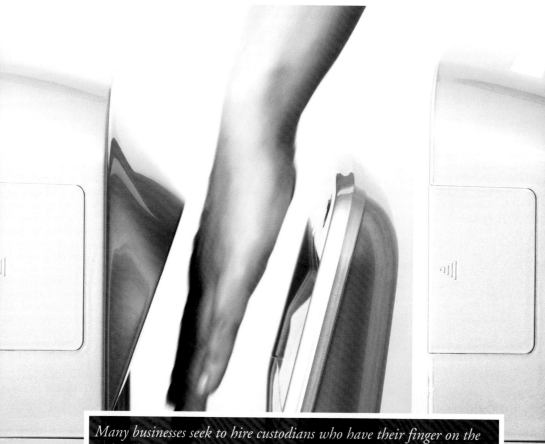

Many businesses seek to hire custodians who have their finger on the pulse of cutting-edge technological advancements. New hand dryers, for examples, dry hands in mere seconds and can save money spent on paper towels.

standing with their hands extended under these contraptions. Janitors who are aware of the newest technology can equip restrooms with powerful hand-drying technology that is incorporated into the faucet itself. The Airblade Tap uses an engine beneath the sink to generate a wind of up to 420 miles (676 kilometers) per hour. Users stay standing in front of the sink to get dry hands. The air is channeled into two wing-like blades on which the users wipe their hands,

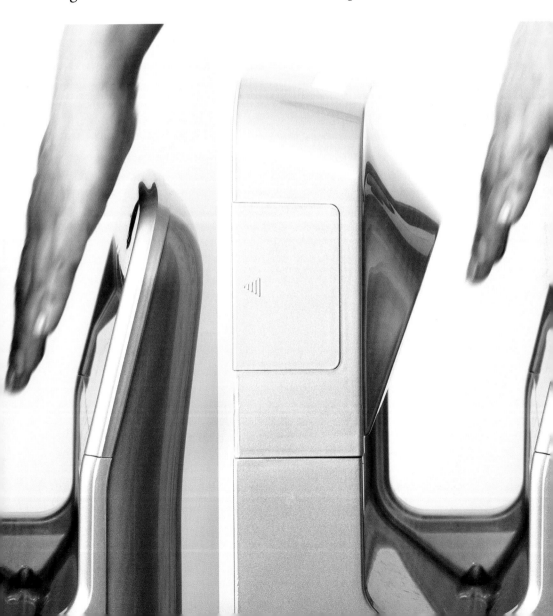

FIGHTING THE JANITOR STEREOTYPE

Professional organizations dedicated to careers in janitorial services are elevating the career to a respected profession. Janitors, however, have often been depicted in movies and television as people who are stupid and subjects of ridicule. The mascot for *Cracked* magazine was a janitor. Groundskeeper Willie on *The Simpsons* seems a bit unhinged. The janitor on the comedy series *Scrubs* and Bill Murray's groundskeeper in the movie *Caddyshack* seemed especially nutty. And, of course, Freddy Krueger is not an ideal role model. In the movie *The Breakfast Club*, one student teases the janitor by asking how you start a career in the "custodial arts." Carl, the janitor, defends the job, saying that he is "the eyes and ears of this institution."

Overall, Carl is favorably portrayed, and several films show the janitor in a positive light. The janitor is favorably portrayed in *The Karate Kid*. He trains the hero in the art of karate so that he can defend himself. In *The Principal*, Louis Gossett Jr. portrays a janitor who genuinely cares for his community. In *Good Will Hunting*, Matt Damon turns out to be a genius janitor and the university where he works gives him a chance to prove himself in the world of academics. The positive janitor role models are out there in television and film, too.

draining excess water into the sink. Employees cut seconds off their bathroom visit so they can get back to their desks sooner and churn out more work. A few seconds might not seem like much, but they add up over the years. And, of course, a hand blower saves on paper towels. Janitors might

Janitors can play an important role on the front lines of public health safety. Their efforts sanitizing hospitals, sports facilities, schools, and other buildings can help stop the spread of disease and illness.

also play a role in installing solar-powered lighting or low-flush toilets that conserve on water usage.

JANITORS ON THE FRONT LINES OF HEALTH

Increasingly, janitors have realized what an important role they play in keeping people healthy. When a norovirus outbreak hit schools in the Clark County district of Nevada, the janitors were called to the rescue, cleaning restrooms and sports facilities to help stop the spread of the illness.

By following news on websites such as the International Janitorial Cleaning Services Association, janitors can keep up with the latest advances in the cleaning industry, meet higher standards of cleanliness, and introduce time-saving and money-saving techniques to benefit the institutions that employ them.

Working in custodial services might seem like a humble way to make a living, but it usually involves more variety and responsibility than people realize. Though we might take it for granted, the importance of keeping spaces clean cannot be overstated. Clean and well-maintained spaces are the key to greater productivity in our workplaces, safety in our schools, and public health in our recreational spaces. Without janitors and the vital role they play, our world would be a lot less pleasant place.

glossary

abrasive A gritty additive in some cleaning products that helps with scouring and scrubbing.

absorbent The ability for a substance to take up fluid.

biodegradable Describes generally organic material that will break down or decompose by biological means, relatively quickly, over time.

buffing Shining a surface with a pad or brush.

compound A mixture of two or more elements that are usually difficult to separate once bonded together, unless by a specific chemical reaction. Many cleaning agents are compounds.

corrosion A chemical reaction that gradually eats away or breaks down a metal surface.

disinfectant A cleaning agent that destroys, stops, or slows the growth of disease-carrying microorganisms.

electrolyzed water A solution of salt and water that is used as a sanitizer.

enzymes Proteins produced in an organism. In cleaning, certain enzymes can actively break down stains, grease, oil, grime, and other types of dirt through biological processes.

finish A protective coating on the surface of a floor that leaves it shiny and easier to clean.

fumigant A gaseous pesticide used for eliminating an infestation of insects.

HVAC Stands for "heating, ventilation, and air-conditioning." This technology controls the air flow, quality, and temperature in an enclosed space.

patina A gloss or sheen.

phosphate A compound containing phosphorous. Phosphates are used in many cleaning products. They have been found to be harmful to the environment.

residue Remains of cleaning agents or dirt left behind after something has been cleaned.

sanitizer A cleaning agent that dramatically decreases bacteria on the area where it is used.

solvent A liquid that dissolves a certain type of substance. Some solvents are used specifically to remove grease, for example.

stripping The process of removing a finish from a hard floor.

varnish A clear, hard, protective finish, mostly used on wood.

for more information

Association of Residential Cleaning Services International (ARCSI)
7870 Olentangy River Road, Suite 301
Columbus, OH 43235
(614) 547-0887
Website: http://www.arcsi.org
ARCSI was established to assist residential cleaning service owners and professionals in starting, promoting, building, and expanding their businesses. Its mission is to provide members with a network of knowledge and experience throughout the industry. By forging these connections, members benefit from new perspectives while also helping to foster profitable growth in the industry.

Canada Cleaning Association
Website: http://www.ijcsacanada.proboards.com
This online bulletin board has various topics related to the cleaning industry, including window washing, carpet cleaning, and floor care.

Canadian Sanitation Supply Association
910 Dundas Street West
P.O. Box 10009
Whitby, ON L1P 1P7
Canada
(905) 665-8001
Website: http://www.cssa.com
This nonprofit promotes a greater public awareness and understanding of sanitary maintenance principles, while

contributing to improved public health and environmental awareness in Canada. The association started a Canadian Green Sustainability Program (CGSP) dedicated to sustainable opportunities and sustainable solutions.

Community College of Allegheny-North Campus
8701 Perry Highway
Pittsburgh, PA 15237
(412) 366-7000
Website: http://www.ccac.edu
The Community College of Allegheny County offers a program in environmental services at its North Campus.

International Building Operators Association
P.O. Box 44166
Boise, ID 83711-0166
(208) 258-3005
Website: http://internationalbuildingoperators.org
This group was formed to enhance and ensure high professional standards, growth, and development of building operators through education, certification, and networking.

International Facility Management Association (IMFA)
800 Gessner Road, Suite 900
Houston, TX 77024-4257
(713) 623-4362
Website: http://www.ifma.org
This organization's mission is to advance the facility management profession. It provides a wide range of educational courses, from entry-level programs to those for highly experienced facility managers.

International Janitorial Cleaning Services Association (IJCSA)
2011 Oak
Wyandotte, MI 48192
(734) 252-6189
Website: http://www.ijcsanetwork.com
IJCSA brings together janitorial services, janitorial suppliers, and
general cleaning services that perform duties such as window
washing, carpet cleaning, and housecleaning. This professional group offers certification in green cleaning, hazardous
chemicals, and more.

International Sanitary Supply Association (ISSA)
7373 N. Lincoln Avenue
Lincolnwood, IL 60712-1799
(800) 225-4772
Website: http://www.issa.com
The source for the professional cleaning industry provides access
to the latest industry news, articles, ISSA-TV educational
videos, and industry management standards.

WEBSITES

Because of the changing nature of Internet links, Rosen Publishing
has developed an online list of websites related to the subject of
this book. This site is updated regularly. Please use this link to
access the list:

http://www.rosenlinks.com/ECAR/Jani

for further reading

Aslett, Don. *The Professional Cleaner's Personal Handbook*. Pocatello, ID: Don Aslett's Cleaning, 2007.

Bewsey, Susan. *Start & Run a Home Cleaning Business*. Bellingham, WA: Self-Counsel Press, 2007.

Bolles, Richard. *What Color Is Your Parachute? 2014: A Practical Manual for Job-Hunters and Career-Changers*. New York, NY: Ten Speed Press, 2013.

Farr, Michael, and Laurence Shatkin. *300 Best Jobs Without a Four-Year Degree*. St. Paul, MN: JIST Works, 2009.

Gordon, Stacey A. *The Successful Interview: 99 Questions to Ask and Answer (and Some You Shouldn't)*. Indianapolis, IN: Diversity Press, 2013.

Hansen, Mark Victor. *The Richest Kids in America: How They Earn It, How They Spend It, How You Can Too*. Newport Beach, CA: Hansen House Publishing, 2009.

Hopkins, Todd, and Ray Hilbert. *The Janitor: How an Unexpected Friendship Transformed a CEO and His Company*. New York, NY: Thomas Nelson/HarperCollins, 2009.

Islam, Sabirul. *Young Entrepreneur World: How 25 Teen-Trepreneurs Succeeded and Left World Leaders Scratching Their Heads*. Singapore: Marshall Cavendish International, 2012.

Lynn, Jacquelyn, and Entrepreneur Press. *Start Your Own Cleaning Service*. Irvine, CA: Entrepreneur Press, 2010.

Morrow, Beth. *How to Open & Operate a Financially Successful Cleaning Service*. Ocala, FL: Atlantic Publishing, 2008.

Murphy, John. *Crafting Competitive Resumes for Teenagers: When You Don't Have Much to Say*. Issaquah, WA: Made for Success, 2009.

Osalor, Peter. *Teenage Entrepreneurs: The Best Time to Start Your Own Business.* London, England: POSAG International Ltd., 2013.

Rose, Riley. *A Killer Resume: The Seven Secret Steps to a Resume That Gets You Hired Every Time* (A Killer Job Search Guide). Seattle, WA: CreateSpace/Amazon, 2013.

Toren, Adam. *Kidpreneurs: Young Entrepreneurs with Big Ideas!* Phoenix, AZ: Business Plus Media Group, 2009.

Tucker, Thomas. *How to Write a Resume: The Resume Writing Book That Helps You Crack Today's Tough Job Market.* Seattle, WA: Amazon Digital Service, 2012.

U.S. Department of Labor. *Occupational Outlook Handbook 2013-2014.* New York, NY: Skyhorse Publishing, 2012.

Vernon, Naomi. *A Teen's Guide to Finding a Job.* Schertz, TX: NU B Publishing, 2013.

Williams, Gabrielle J. *The Making of a Young Entrepreneur: A Kid's Guide to Developing the Mind-Set for Success.* Bowie, MD: Legacy Builder Group, 2011.

Yate, Martin. *Knock 'em Dead 2013: The Ultimate Job Search Guide.* Avon, MA: Adams Media, 2012.

Zelinski, Ernie J. *Career Success Without a Real Job: The Career Book for People Too Smart to Work in Corporations.* Edmonton, AB: Visions International Publishing, 2009.

bibliography

Aziz, John. "Is This Self-Cleaning Plate the Future of Eating?" *The Week,* December 24, 2013. Retrieved March 20, 2014 (http://theweek.com/article/index/254558/is-this-self -cleaning-plate-the-future-of-eating).

Bureau of Labor Statistics. "Janitors and Building Cleaners." *Occupational Outlook Handbook,* January 8, 2014. Retrieved March 20, 2014 (http://www.bls.gov/ooh/ building-and-grounds-cleaning/janitors-and-building -cleaners.htm#tab-3).

CareerDepot.org. "Janitors and Cleaners, Except Maids and Housekeeping Cleaners." Retrieved March 20, 2013 (http://www.careerdepot.org/Descriptions/job _janitor.htm).

Cashill, Margaret. "AFS Janitorial Cleans Up Around Florida." *Tampa Bay Business Journal,* February 17, 2012. Retrieved March 20, 2013 (http://www .bizjournals.com/tampabay/print-edition/2012/ 02/17/afs-janitorial-cleans-up-around-florida.html ?page=all).

CVTips. "Janitor Jobs—Jobs as a Janitor." Retrieved March 20, 2014 (http://www.cvtips.com/career-choice/janitorial -jobs---jobs-as-a-janitor.html).

DailyKos. "Jobs That Matter—Janitors." September 4, 2014. Retrieved March 20, 2013 (http://www.dailykos.com/ story/2013/09/05/1235182/-Jobs-that-matter-Janitors).

Huang, Menglin. "Job Opportunities for Youth? Report Points to Janitorial Services." *MetroFocus*, June 12, 2012. Retrieved March 20, 2014 (http://www.thirteen.org/ metrofocus/2012/06/for-unemployed-youth-rethinking -janitor-jobs).

International Janitorial Cleaning Services Association. "Recent Cleaning News." Retrieved March 20, 2014 (http://www.ijcsanetwork.com/Industry-News).

International Sanitary Supply Association. "Cleaning Industry Management Standard." Retrieved March 20, 2014 (http://www.issa.com/?id=cleaning_industry_management_standard_cims).

Krall, Daniel. "Green Cleaning Trends: Cleaning with Electrolyzed Water." *Today's Facility Manager,* October 2013. Retrieved March 20, 2014 (http://todaysfacilitymanager.com/2013/11/green-cleaning-trends-cleaning-electrolyzed-water).

McGowan, Bailey. "Tools of Love: Couple Runs Crime Scene Cleaning Business Together." KHOU, September 4, 2013. Retrieved March 20, 2014 (http://www.khou.com/news/texas-news/Tools-of-Love-Couple-runs-crime-scene-cleaning-business-together-222428451.html).

McKenna, Maryn. "Clean Sweep: Hospitals Bring Janitors to the Frontlines of Infection Control." *Scientific American,* August 15, 2012. Retrieved March 20, 2014 (http://www.scientificamerican.com/article/hospitals-bring-janitors-front-lines-of-infection-control).

Moyer, Mike. "My Entrepreneurial Story." *Mike for Short,* December 13, 2010. Retrieved March 20, 2014 (http://www.mikeforshort.com/my-entrepreneurial-story-part-1).

MyMajors. "School Janitor." Retrieved March 20, 2014 (http://www.mymajors.com/careers-and-jobs/school-janitor).

Quigley, Rachel. "How 'Flamin' Hot Cheetos' Transformed Immigrant Janitor Without a High School Degree into a Corporate Executive." MailOnline, October 16, 2013. Retrieved March 20, 2013 (http://www.dailymail.co.uk/news/article-2463533/How-Flamin-Hot-Cheetos-transformed-immigrant-janitor-high-school-degree-corporate-executive.html).

Saidi, Nicole. "Overheard on CNN.com: Teen Janitor's Story 'Like Good Will Hunting,' Readers Say." CNN, June 7, 2012. Retrieved March 20, 2014 (http://news.blogs.cnn .com/2012/06/07/overheard-on-cnn-com-teen-janitors -story-like-good-will-hunting-readers-say).

Sustainable Supply. "Cleaning & Janitorial." Retrieved March 20, 2014 (http://www.sustainablesupply.com/Green -Cleaning-Products-Green-Janitorial-Supplies-s/1.htm).

US News & World Report. "Janitor." Retrieved March 20, 2014 (http://money.usnews.com/careers/best-jobs/janitor).

Vaughan, Vicki. "Janitorial Services Firm Built on Sweat Equity, Penny-Pinching." *San Antonio Express-News*, December 10, 2013. Retrieved March 20, 2013 (http:// www.expressnews.com/business/local/article/Janitorial -services-firm-built-on-sweat-equity-5052781.php).

WikiHow. "How to Start a Successful Janitorial Service." Retrieved March 20, 2014 (http://www.wikihow.com/Start -a-Successful-Janitorial-Service).

index

A

ABM Janitorial Services, 36
Airblade Tap, 63–64
American School and
    University, 42
Angie's List, 50
apprenticeships, 40, 45, 47

B

bookkeeping, 14
BotVac, 62
budgeting, 21, 53
Bureau of Labor Statistics, 5, 16,
    18, 43

C

Carpenter, Lawrence, 50
carpentry, 48, 51
Carrey, Jim, 6
celebrities that have been janitors,
    6, 25
certification, 6, 26, 40–42
Cleaning Industry Management
    Standard certification, 40
Community College of Allegheny
    County, 42
computer knowledge, 21, 40
Crime Clean of Texas, 31
crime-scene cleanup, 31

E

education, 40, 42–43, 44–47, 48
electricians/electrical work, 5, 13,
    18, 19, 26, 44–45, 47, 48
employment services, 36
equipment, using specialized, 6,
    13, 19, 26, 27, 39, 60–65
ergonomics, 18

G

"green" cleaning practices, 6, 9,
    57–60
Groupon, 50

H

Haines, Larry, 51–52
HVAC (heating, ventilation, and
    air-conditioning), 13, 26, 44,
    47–48

I

illnesses, preventing spread of,
    16, 21, 27, 29, 57–59, 65–66
Indeed, 36
International Executive
    Housekeepers Association, 42
International Janitorial Cleaning
    Services Association, 42,
    60, 66

International Sanitary Supply
    Association, 42, 60
internships, 36, 40
interviews, questions asked and
    mistakes made during,
    38–39

J

janitorial and cleaning services
    careers
    advancing in, 5, 42–56
    duties of, 10, 13–16, 19–29
    getting started in, 32–43
    latest developments in, 57–66
    locations of jobs, 25–31
    making money and succeeding in,
        7–10, 34–35, 50–51
    need for, 5, 10, 44, 65–66
    outlook and job growth, 5, 16
    pros/benefits of, 5, 16
    qualities needed, 23–25
    risks of, 18
    salaries, 43
    self-quiz for, 12–13
    starting your own business, 32,
        50–51
    stereotypes of, 64
    tools of the trade, 22–23, 60–65
    training and education for,
        36–37, 40–43, 44–47, 48

K

King, Stephen, 6
Koster, Bart, 25

L

Langone Medical Center, 29
Loggins, Dawn, 32, 36

M

Maid Brigade, 36
Manpower, 36
Montañez, Richard, 54–56
Moore, Charles, 31
Moore, Deborah, 31
Moyer, Mike, 9–10

N

National Association of Certified
    Building Contractors, 42
New York University, 29

O

Occupational Safety and Health
    Administration, 47

P

plumbing, 13, 19, 26, 44, 45, 47

R

Raver, Bryson, 7–9, 10
recycling, 6, 57, 59
Reeves, Keanu, 6
résumé tips, 26
Reznor, Trent, 25
Robbins, Tony, 6

S

safety and safety training, 18, 22, 47, 57–59
security guards, 14
SnagaJob, 36
Super Clean Professional Janitorial Services, 50
superintendents of buildings, 5, 52–53
Superior Cleaning Company, 7
supplies, managing and ordering, 14–15, 21

T

360 Facility Services, Inc., 7–8
training courses, 36–37, 40, 44–47, 48

U

unions, 36, 43, 45
U.S. Department of Labor, 39, 40

W

Worldwide Cleaning Industry Association, 40–42, 60

ABOUT THE AUTHOR

Don Rauf was the editor in chief of *Careers and Colleges* magazine. Rauf has written many books on career success.

PHOTO CREDITS

Cover, p. 1 (figure) AndreyPopov/iStock/Thinkstock; cover, p. 1 (background) zhu difeng/Shutterstock.com; pp. 4–5 kurhan/Shutterstock.com; pp. 8–9 Kathleen Cabble/Tampa Bay Business Journal; p. 11 Stock Connection/SuperStock; p. 14–15, 46–47 auremar/Shutterstock.com; p. 17 ChrisWindson/Photodisc/Getty Images; p. 20 Oskari Porkka/Shutterstock.com; p. 24 Blaj Gabriel/Shutterstock.com; pp. 28–29 Matthew Brown/E+/Getty Images; pp. 30–31 Foto24/Gallo Images/Getty Images; p. 33 Charlotte Observer/McClathy-Tribune/Getty Images; pp. 36–37 Andrey_Popov/Shutterstock.com; p. 41 Community College of Allegheny County; pp. 48–49 Blend Images/Dream Pictures/Getty Images; pp. 52–53 dotshock/Shutterstock.com; pp. 54–55 Ryan Miller/Invision/AP Images; pp. 58–59 Steve Winter/National Geographic Image Collection/Getty Images; p. 61 Yoshikazu Tsuno/AFP/Getty Images; pp. 62–63 Tiramisu Studio/Shutterstock.com; p. 65 Getty Images.

Designer: Matt Cauli; Editor: Christine Poolos;
Photo Researcher: Marty Levick